NOT ALL GOATS HAVE HORNS

There's a popular misconception that females do not grow horns but in reality both males and females can grow horns. If a goat is missing their horn then, either the goat has been disbudded or dehorned, or it was naturally born without one.

HORN SHAPES

The horn of a goat varies on on the breed. Sometimes in rare cases a goat can have more than two horns, which means the goat is polycerate. But four horns is normal for the Austrian goat breed, Vierhornziege.

GOATS ARE VERY AGILE

Goats have slim bodies that let them get over ledges and squeeze next to rocks. Their hooves are split into two sections. It allows them to spread the halves to grip a larger rock surface. The bottoms of their hooves have rubbery pads. The pads provided the goats with even more traction.

GOAT AS A PET?

when a goat is domesticated, they are sometimes used as pets. They are friendly and very therapeutic to people. Beware, goats do smell!

GOAT TEETH

Goats only have bottom teeth. The top teeth are just gums. Goats have evolved to lack top front teeth because they proved to be an unnecessary part of their digestive process.

GOAT COLORS

Goats can come with hundreds of color combinations and patterns alone its entire body. Black, red or tan are the most common colors, any of which may be in combination with white.

GOAT FOOD

Most goats prefer weeds and grass. Even though they mainly eat hay, weeds, and grass, goats will also eat a wide verity of foods like fruits, bread, and vegetables. Although goats are herbivores, they might steal a slice of meat from you if your not careful!

RAIN AND WATER

Goats hate getting wet! Either from weather and rain or just standing still in side of it, goats do not seem to like it. Goats can swim with a doggy paddle like motion, but they would not choose to do it very willingly.

BABY GOATS

Baby goats are very cute and friendly (for the most part). They don't normally grow their horns until they're two weeks old. Baby goats are also called kids! Baby goats are born without any teeth, their first teeth start to come through once they are about one week old.

GOATS STOMACH

The goat's stomach has four chambers, the rumen, the honeycombed reticulum, the omasum, and the abomasum stomach. The size and the chambers of these different stomachs will change in size differently as the goat grows.

GOATS CLEAN?

Goats are considered clean animals because of their eating habits. most goats eat more woody plant material. To be considered clean you need to be healthy, have a good diet, clean water and proper home care. Because goats can be picky eaters sometimes, this helps keep them clean

GOAT SOUNDS

Just like humans and many other animals, you can tell what a goat wants based on how it presents its tone. Goats have different sounds to let you know about something, either if its hungry, tired, happy, or irritated.

GOAT MILK

Goat milk is the best alternative to regular milk. It is naturally more nutritious than a lot of other milks based on studies. Goat milk is a lot easier to digest for the human body. Goat milk has higher levels of protein, calcium, and phosphorus.

GOATS LIFE SPAM

The natural life expectancy of a goat is 10 to 15 years. Sometimes a goat can reach up to 18-20 years of age with proper care and good health. A lot of goats don't make it past 7 - 8 years of age because of health problems, commonly in the teeth.

GOATS EYES

A Goats pupils are rectangular. This gives them vision for 320 to 340 degrees (compared to humans with 160-210) around them without having to move and have excellent night vision abilities.

TICS

Goats produce natural oils in their hair to help prevent ticks. This doesn't work 100% of the time. If a goat is tick infested then the goat would have skin irritation, damage to the skin and hide, limping and wound development.

GOAT ORIGIN

Goat remains have been first found 10,000 years ago in Iran. Goat remains have also been found at archaeological sites in Jericho, Choga Mami, Djeitun, and Çayönü, dating back between 8,000 and 9,000 years ago

WHO HAS MORE GOATS?

Asia is home to most goats in the world, followed by Africa. Africa is home to more than 40% of the world's goat population. In recent studies they are saying that china has over 170 Million goats reaching over the amount of Asia and Africa. There are over 1 billion goats around the world!

WHAT DOES FAMILY MEAN TO MOTHER GOATS?

Sadly sometimes the mother doesn't want to bond with her kid after the weaning process. In other cases the mother is accepting of her baby into the family.

FEMALE GOATS

Female goats can get pregnant for up to 12 years of age. A female goat is called a doe or nanny. female goat giving birth is called kidding. Just like males, Females can grow beards.

SOCIAL CREATURES

Goats are social creatures and they like to be in herds with other goats. If you ever consider getting a goat as a pet or farm animal, it will need proper attention.

BALANCE

Goats have excellent balance due to there hooves and it is not uncommon to see them climb trees and steep rock walls. Although most goats can climb very well, not all goats have the same confidence to do so.

SMILE

They say goats prefer a happy face and not a frowny face. Goats are social animals and tend to read body language from a human very well. Goats interact with positive body language the best when smiling

GOATS ARE GREAT AT DIETS

Goats can survive on the thinnest patches of grass. They also eat tree sticky foods like tree bark and hay. Tree bark is rick in tannins. Goats are picky eaters but also are capable of eating and chewing most things.

WHERE ARE GOATS SO FRIENDLY?

over 9,000 years ago, ancestors would use these animals and 'train' them. Either using these animals as livestock or using them to transport heavy possessions long distances. This being part of a goats routine caused them to be naturally obedient and friendly today.

EYE POSITIONING

Goat have side slanted eyes, which typically belong to grazing prey, giving them a wider frame of view. This helps them not get too much sunlight directly in their eyes and makes it easier for them to keep an eye out for predators.

EMOTIONS?

Goats are extremely smart and can be very preceptive. Goats are able to learn things in only a matter of a couple attempts. They also make noises and sounds to present how they are feeling in a situation, or stressful environment.

MYTHOLOGY?

Thor, the god of thunder, typically walked or used his hammer to fly. But according to Norse mythology, during a thunderstorm Thor rode in a chariot pulled by TWO GOATS, Tanngrisnir and Tanngnjóstr.

FAINTING GOATS?

Goats don't actually faint when they get frightened or startled. Their legs freeze up and go into a shock like state, but they are completely conscious. This is a Skeletal Muscle condition called myotonia. So no, goats don't just faint for no reason.

LEGENDS OF COFFEE

Legend goes that coffee was discovered after a goat herder in Ethiopia noticed that his goats became energized and wouldn't sleep after they were spotted eating berries from a particular tree. After sharing his discovery, drinks began to be made with these mysterious berries, and the knowledge of these energizing beans spread across the world.

Printed in Great Britain
by Amazon